Rocky and the Wolf Cub

Written by Sherryl Clark
Illustrated by Andy Elkerton

mountains
cave
forest
animal track
river
village

Contents

A Strange Noise

Rocky groaned. He hated going to gather nuts and berries for his mum. He'd much rather be playing down by the river with his friend, Stubb. Maybe if he hurried, he could still play before dark.

He ran into the forest, along the track made by animals. He remembered what his dad told him – always keep an eye out. You never know when you might come across a bear or a wolf pack.

Every now and then, Rocky stopped to pick berries. Suddenly, just off the track, he spotted a hazelnut tree. Its ripe nuts had fallen to the ground. Good! He could fill the bag and run home again.

Rocky knelt down and scooped up handfuls of nuts.

A strange noise made Rocky look up. There in the bushes, not far away, two eyes gleamed.

Rocky froze. What was it? A bear? A wild pig?

The noise came again – a sad whine and a tiny yelp. It sounded like a wolf cub.

Rocky jumped up and stared around. Where was the mother wolf? She might leap out at any moment and attack him.

He waited, holding his breath, but nothing happened.

Slowly, slowly, he stepped towards the bush and the eyes. Something smelt bad so he tried not to breathe.

He parted the leaves and saw a mother wolf, lying behind the bush. She was dead. Beside her sat a little cub – all alone.

Chapter 2

Alf

What should Rocky do? He couldn't abandon the cub, but he'd get into trouble if he took it into the village.

The cub whimpered again and crawled towards Rocky, its nose on its paws.

That did it. Rocky bent down and gently scooped it up. The cub didn't growl or bite, so he tucked it inside his tunic. The cub's fur tickled Rocky's skin as the cub curled up and went to sleep.

Rocky hurried back to the village. He hoped no one would see him.

Smoke from the evening cooking fires filled the air. Mum was busy gutting a large fish, so Rocky scooted into the hut while her back was turned. The cub hardly moved as he tucked it under his sleeping fur.

"Good boy," said Mum when she saw the bag of nuts. "Take this stone and bowl and crush them for me."

She carefully placed the fish onto the cooking stones to bake. While Dad was away hunting, Rocky had to give Mum more help.

Later, as they ate, Rocky hid pieces of fish for the cub. He worried that the cub would wake up and jump out of the hut, but it stayed fast asleep.

When Rocky fed it the fish, the cub growled and pounced on it as though it was still alive! The cub made funny little "woof" noises.

"I'm going to call you Alf," said Rocky. Alf grinned a toothy grin at him.

Chapter 3

The Secret

That night, Rocky kept Alf with him under his sleeping fur. Alf wriggled and scratched, and Rocky wriggled and scratched too.

It was late into the night when Rocky finally slept, and long after dawn when he woke up.

Oh no! Where was Alf?

There he was, on the other side of the hut, dragging Mum's sleeping fur around. Rocky jumped up and grabbed the fur. Alf growled.

"Shh!" Rocky whispered. He reached for his deerskin boots but they were all chewed up and covered in wolf spit. Mum would be so angry!

Rocky had to get the cub out of the hut. He tucked Alf inside his tunic again and ran to Stubb's hut in bare feet.

Stubb was drawing pictures on a large rock with a blackened stick from the fire.

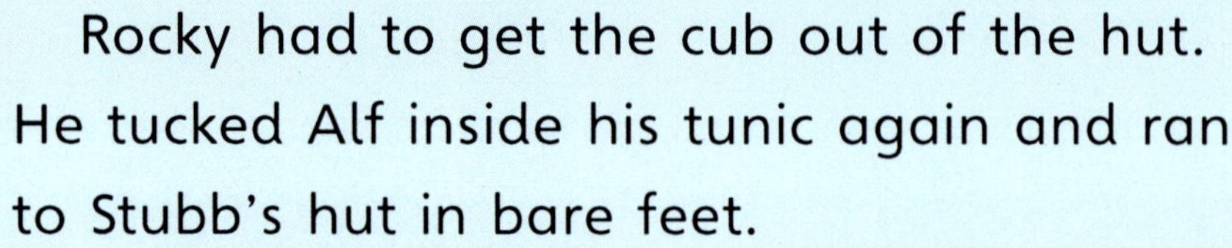

"What's the matter with your stomach?" asked Stubb, pointing.

"It's not me. It's a wolf," said Rocky.

Stubb laughed. "That's funny." But he stopped laughing when Alf poked his head out of the tunic. "Does your mum know you've got that?"

Rocky shook his head. "And he's just chewed up my boots. Have you got a spare pair?"

"No, sorry," said Stubb.

Rocky didn't know what to do with the cub. He had to hide it, he had to feed it, and he had to stop it chewing their furs.

Stubb was no help – he just laughed. Rocky knew he should take Alf back to the forest, but when Alf nuzzled up under his chin, and he felt Alf's little heart beating, he just couldn't do it.

So Rocky took Alf back to the hut and pushed him down under his sleeping fur.

"Stay there and keep quiet!" he said.

Alf just stuck out his tongue and waggled it.

Chapter 4

Big Trouble

"Rocky!" called Mum. "Please skin and gut this rabbit. Then put it on this big stick over the fire to cook."

Rocky did as she said and the rabbit was soon sizzling. He checked in the hut. Alf was fast asleep, so Rocky went down to the river to fish. He balanced his sharpened spear above him and got ready for a fish to come out of the shadows.

"Rocky!" Mum shouted. She was waving madly at him. Rocky ran back to the hut.

"Look!" said Mum, pointing at the empty stick. "Our roasted rabbit is missing! We've got nothing else to eat."

Rocky had a horrible feeling that he knew where it might be, but he didn't say anything. He helped Mum to look for the rabbit.

Mum soon spotted a leg bone lying on the ground, and then another. They followed the trail to the back of the hut ...

... where they found Alf crouched over the remains of the rabbit.

Mum roared, "Get out of here, you hairy thief!"

Alf bolted, skidding around the corner of the hut and out of sight.

Mum glared at Rocky. "Where did that come from? Did you bring it from the forest?"

"The cub was all alone," said Rocky. "Its mother was dead."

"So will that cub be, if I get my hands on it!" said Mum.

Rocky walked back to the cooking fire behind Mum. He was very hungry, and he knew that he'd be in big trouble when Dad got back! But worst of all, Alf was gone. He'd probably run back to the forest and was lost by now. He was so young that he wouldn't last long alone.

Rocky slumped down with a sad heart and stirred the fire with a big stick.

"I'll have to use some of our stored food," grumbled Mum, heading back into their hut.

Suddenly, she screamed so loudly that Rocky leapt up like he'd been burnt.

"Mum! What's wrong?" he cried. He ran to the doorway of the hut. Mum was backed up against the opposite side. A huge green snake was heading straight for her, hissing angrily.

"Get the axe!" Mum shouted.

But just as Rocky grabbed the axe, Alf ran past and jumped onto the snake, gripping its head with his teeth.

Rocky tried to aim, but Alf's paws were in the way.

Rocky dodged this way ...

and that way ...

until ...

… the snake's head was off. Alf shook it a few times then spat it out.

"Goodness me!" Mum gasped. "You saved me, Rocky. Brave boy."

"No, Alf saved us," said Rocky. He scratched Alf behind his ears and grinned at his mum. "You should pat him and say thanks."

Mum nervously gave Alf one quick pat.

"Can he stay now?" Rocky asked. "Please?"

Mum looked at the dead snake. "I suppose so, but only until your father gets back. Then we'll see."

Rocky smiled. He was happy with that – for now.